THE WINDMILL PROOF

THE WINDMILL PROOF

Stephen Payne

HAPPENSTANCE

BY THE SAME AUTHOR:

Pattern Beyond Chance, Happen*Stance*, 2015
The Probabilities of Balance, Smiths Knoll pamphlet, 2010

ACKNOWLEDGEMENTS:

Some of these poems, or earlier versions, appeared in the following journals: *The Dark Horse, The Lonely Crowd, Magma, The North, Poetry Wales, The Rialto.* Some were included in *The Probabilities of Balance* (*Smiths Knoll*, 2010).

Italicised phrases in 'Point', Line', 'and 'Cylinder' are quotations from Euclid's *Elements (*trans. Thomas Little Heath).Those in 'Cone' are quotations from his *Optics* (trans. Harry Edwin Burton), as is the epigraph.

The Laura Kasischke poem mentioned in 'Lines in Denver' is 'For the Young Woman I Saw Hit by a Car While Riding Her Bike'.

'clammy cell' in 'Hexagon' is from John Keats's 'To Autumn'.

'things being various' in 'The Riddle of the Buddhist Monk' is drawn from Louis MacNeice's 'Snow'.

'The Nylon Tent' takes its pattern from Robert Frost's 'The Silken Tent'.

Many thanks to my poetry friends & teachers in Cardiff & Bath & beyond, & to all members of the Poetry Business Writing School 2017–2018.

NOTE FOR VISUALLY IMPAIRED READERS:

The jacket colour is pale grey. The front jacket bears a diagram illustrating Pythagoras's theorem by means of a right-angled triangle with sides of three different lengths. Each triangle side forms the basis of an adjacent square & looks not unlike a windmill. The thick lines of the 'windmill' are faded red. The author's name (dark red) is placed inside the bottom (small) square. The book title is below this in dark mauve, though the two Os of 'PROOF' are red. The back jacket has a descriptive paragraph, two quotes from critics re. the poet's previous book, and a sample poem ('Triangle', p. 21). Text of quotes & poem is dark red. Other text is dark mauve. The inside jacket, front and back, is patterned with geometrical shapes & mathematical equations.

First published in 2021 by Happen*Stance* Press
21 Hatton Green, Glenrothes KY7 4SD
https://happenstancepress.com
ISBN: 978-1-910131-60-2

The maths graphic (inside front & back jackets) was obtained from depositphotos.com

Printed & bound by Imprint Digital, Exeter
https://digital.imprint.co.uk

CONTENTS

Euclid alone has looked on Beauty bare.

—Edna St. Vincent Millay

Nothing that is seen is seen at once in its entirety.

—Euclid

THE BIG LEAP

—i.m. Peter Payne, 17.12.1929–19.02.2019

For me, you'll always be mid-air
above the garden pond
you leapt across
from a standing start
when we were playing tag.
None of us kids breathed.
The goldfishes looked up, open-mouthed.

POINT

X or a dot
marks the spot.
It's where it's at.
Pure place,
no space for even
a single angel.
The end of the line
and the beginning.
That which has no part,
the atom
of Euclid's eye.

LINES IN DENVER

A corrugated curlicue
of pickups' tyre tracks in the snow
outside the café. Now
my footprints too.

Ten minutes later I'm blinking back tears,
reading a poem by Laura Kasischke
about a crash. A car
maybe oversteers

and hits a bicycle.
The girl knocked from her bike is fine
but the poem contemplates the line
not crossed: how close a call,

how beautiful the breakable and frail.
I settle up and set off on a walk
to John F. Kennedy park
along the Cherry Creek Trail.

The trees are almost bare.
A few brown-paper leaves are all
the mile-high Colorado fall
has deigned to spare.

The fallen snow is swirling through the air.

LINE

A breadthless length.

Drawn, it's a model

of something finer, more abstract,

diagonal, curve, tangent to the curve,

the edge of a surface,

figure/ground,

geometry/art.

Also a model of a real path:

incident light refracting through a lens;

a chain between two hooks;

the reader's gaze, following an idea.

SWITCH

At Temple Meads, train front became train back.
Until this midway change of tack

I was considering the here
in terms of what was drawing near.

Now I face what lies behind.
There goes the Avon, sedge-and-hawthorn-lined

and there, beyond my window-ghost,
a narrowboat, already lost.

Further downriver, Bristol's time
is on my mind again, that chime

of digits on the platform clock;
also a time of life, a chapter. Look—

I'm there with Ros on the suspension bridge
watching the dawn return the wooded ridge.

PLANE

At school we learned
to tessellate it
with regular polygons

and that three points
determine a plane
which is why a milking stool
has three legs
even though a cow has four.

Like a school rule,
something about
its stretched-skin essence
makes it hard to contemplate
without imagining it
broken.

We learned to define
the plane of a window
with a cricket ball.

A plane is a surface
where deep stuff happens.
Euclid breathed on the glass
and drew with his finger
a map of shapes

then wrote his name.

HOLES

Arsehole
bolthole
cubbyhole

in a deep hole

porthole pinhole pupil Polo
piss-hole in the snow

hole in my bucket
hole in my heart

zero's prototypes

ontology's joke
now you see them
now you don't

essentially immaterial

apertures and lacunae
freedom and loss

punch them
prick them
try to fix them
worry them with your tongue

freedom and loss

perfect mates
on touching they become one
punning itself
greater than the sum of its parts

ORIGAMI

This is art but not sculpture
so much as mathematics.
A sheet of paper, cut square,
offers theorems about

its latent third dimension:
that it contains a dragon-
fly, or a boat. Every
fold is a step of a proof.

A new theorem, therefore,
concerning you, lovely girl,
sitting at your bedroom desk,
absorbed in your handiwork:

that you are both an artist
and a mathematician
in the making. Every
fold is a step of a proof.

ANGLE

I'm writing this
at 51.42 degrees north,
3.19 degrees west.
Once you can measure angles
you know where you are
and you can navigate by the stars.
Give that boy a protractor!

It's where two lines meet,
   and where things get practical.
It's where mathematics
   meets architecture.

It's where the leg meets the foot.
A right ankle
         is one that lets you stand up straight.

SHAVE

I cut myself more since I switched
to a safety razor made
in Sheffield from Sheffield steel
with a classic double-edge blade.

I like that I'm slower
each morning at the mirror,
needing to lather up some soap
and shape my face, my own finger

marking the line of my mouth
as if I were both snowman
and snowman maker—
the one who melts in the sun

and the one who grows old
in all his flesh and blood.

THIS POEM IS ABOUT SELF-REFERENCE

Think hard
about the word *word*
and you're down
in the dirt
with Kurt Gödel
and Bertrand Russell.
It is what it is.
Things get weird
when language talks
about itself.
This be the verse.
This sentence
is not true.
Or that cartoon
in *The Beano*,
a sign bearing
a single order:
Do not throw stones
at this notice.
It's a favourite of mine
for cocking a snook
at dumb officialdom
and for making me laugh
even now
at me and Paul laughing.

THE MOUSETAIL MAN

I noticed him in the distance down the lane.
His coat and cap were similar to mine
but as he approached I saw this man was older,
his face more written on by trouble and weather.
He stopped and said, *You just passed a rare plant.*
We tracked back to a gate. *I'll have to hunt.*
It only grows on ground pounded by cattle.
I spotted it here last spring. It's called Mousetail.
It was some time before he found a patch,
a few thin stalks, the tiny flower on each
tipping it whitely but unshowily.
He said, *I came here today, especially*
and it occurred to me that I did too.
When we shook hands, he smiled as if he knew.

TRIANGLE

The geometer said
Let trigons be trigons
but 'triangle' it stays

for a pointy polygon,
arrowhead and instrument,
metaphor and sign

pointing to inequality,
the priority
of the straight line.

The sum of the lengths
of any two sides
is greater than the length of the third

so if Alex loves Blake and Blake loves Chris
it would be easier
if Alex loves Chris.

IN MY DREAMS

Enter my teenage son,
arriving home late.
He tiptoes across the bedroom
to kiss me as I sleep.

COMMUTE

After the tunnel my mind begins to wander
and all my wonderings are so interior
that when I peer out through the carriage window
nothing is even distantly familiar
until that church beside the factory
not only tells me exactly where we are
but helps to dissipate the prior blur,
leaving as a different mystery
why things have been initially obscure.

SQUARE

A nightingale sang in Berkeley rectangle.
A square is a rectangle
though a rectangle
aint necessarily square.

A square is a rhombus, though, et cetera.
And a square is a parallelogram.
You could say a square
is a special case,

a set intersection,
a meeting place.
Like Berkeley Square
where the nightingale sang.

WALKING IN SÃO CARLOS

1. Praça XV de Novembro

It's already tomorrow.
Emboldened by red wine
I'm crossing the square
named for the day in 1889
when the army deposed the emperor.

Street lights spread shadows
of empty benches
across the gravel perimeter.

And here's a local citizen
awake at this strange, small hour,
breathing the perfumes
of a lemon tree in his front yard.
He's wearing shorts, a black fedora
and the same magnificent moustaches
as those of Machado de Assis
on the back of my *Dom Casmurro.*

He waves an elaborate wave, as if
to write me into his story

and I wave back.

2. Rua Padre Teixeira

A bike clanks past, with a contraption
pushed in front, cart before iron horse.
Squashed inside is a boy, his bare feet
inches above the burn of tarmac.
The cyclist (the boy's dad I'm guessing)
is orchestrating some kind of game.
Once every block he raises a hand
and bellows a single-word command
to the junior member of the team
who responds with a full-blooded scream.

3. Avenida Dr Carlos Botelho

Hot, hot day. Two o'clock.
The streets are choked with traffic
and the legislators of this city block
are three dogs, riding on the back
of a battered pickup truck.
The dogs are sinewed and black
and they bark and they bark.
They bark at the cars parked
at the roadside, they bark
at the drugstore and the supermarket,
at the petrol station and the bank.
At the juggler on the crossroads, the arc
of his clubs, his golden arms, they bark.

4. Avenida São Carlos

The smile of a teenage girl hurrying
for the bus you passed, oblivious, a few
forgotten thoughts ago on your way back
from the cathedral where what used to be
an open square for families to gather
is now a parking lot;

                                        the way she seemed
to laugh both at herself and at a world
that maybe had caught her out, or maybe not;

the glance shared with her friend that says they walked
a little too slowly or talked a little too much
but hey, that's just the way they are together;

the moment they noticed the people at the stop
would surely keep the bus waiting long enough.

All this in a couple of paces but carried the whole
way back to your hotel. Doesn't it make
everything better, if only for a while?

HEXAGON

Everybody needs hexagon
in their lexicon, what with its
perfect number of sides

and symmetries.
The regular guy
is the special one,

the footprint of carbon
in those textbook diagrams
of organic compounds

and the clammy cell
that makes us all wax lyrical.
Honeyed tessellator,

it's fit for what's built,
bearing more weight
with less matter.

It's part of the pattern.
It's the nut
and the bolt.

THE POOL

For length after length
I have bubbled my worries
into the turquoise.

Now I sit in the foyer,
lording it over the indecision
of automatic doors.

A boy at my table cradles a gift
of vending-machine hot chocolate
but as he lifts the cup to his lips
he shivers at some passing thought
and a ripple of chocolate spills.

Without even taking a sip
he places the cup on the table
so as completely to cover
the small dark pool.

MISC.

How to say it,
this abbreviation? Whisper
(or squint) and it's like Mix,

the meaning of its origin
in Latin, which takes me back
to Mr Wakeling's classroom,

its glimpse of the sky, its view
over the tennis courts toward the girls' school,
the legendary rule

declaring that boys and girls
must not have intercourse
through the netting of the boundary fence

and the thirty or so of us
in class 2R—
R for *Romani*—conjugating

amo amas amat ... in unison,
perhaps all of us wondering, like me,
if we'll ever fall in love

and whether we belong here—
preferring, instead, to count ourselves
among the miscellaneous,

the allsorts and outsiders;
not merely uncategorisable,
but anti-bureaucratic,

exposing a broken scheme,
and dissing, really,
the whole idea of schemes.

Hooray for the things that are labelled
only by what they are not:
the unidentified flying objects.

OVERCONFIDENCE

Ninety per cent of start-ups fold.
Most engineering projects come in over budget
and late. More than half of all marriages

end in divorce.
Tell me some jokes. Too many are not funny.
Too many strawberries get eaten by slugs.

The minister has announced
that as a matter of policy
most schools will be above average.

And indeed (studies have shown) most pupils believe
they themselves already are.
Who expects to come bottom of the class?

We must travel hopefully.
It's good to remember the Panama Canal,
Paul Newman and Joanne Woodward,

Django Reinhardt. And our student,
the one who went on to achieve
the lowest mark.

How he puzzled over
that especially tricky question
posed during the first class of the year.

Perhaps he looked up from the page
to the faces of his classmates,
their studious expressions,

and set himself a modest target
—say somewhere in the top two-thirds—
not so much overconfident, as willing

but unable to predict the distractions of the city,
the snags at the junctions
between his and his teachers' ways of thinking.

THE RIVER SWIMMER

He dips his toe, endures the creeping shock
with each slow stride, the goose-bumps and the shivers.
He curses as the crooked light
tells lies about a rock.
All this to swim—to fight
upstream toward the source,
testing his strength against the river's—
then to be still, to tread
the pool's deep water so its whorls
can rinse away his trouble.
He slips his ring and watches as it falls,
dives steeply into an amber blur to fetch.
Or fail. A sudden panic of remorse
until—a glint of gold—his fingers stretch...
Breathing relief, he feels the bubbles bubble
past his upward-floating hair
and pushes from the riverbed
to race the last ones back to air.

ALMA MATER

1. Winter playground
so
cold
you
could

make
slides
black
ice

slick
all
week
till

the
thaw

2. Foggy bashing week
first
years'
worst
fears

billiard
balls
toilet
bowls

stuff
of
legend

nothing
ever
happened

3. Motto

pas
à
pas
on
va
bien
loin

was
a
less-
on
few
boys
learned

4. Rugby

those
grunty
winter
hours
centres
froze
front
rows
never
steam
hovered
over
every
scrum

5. Woodwork report

saw
loser
loose
bored

holes
and
ruined
dowels

didn't
auger
well

made
bugger
all

THE RIDDLE OF THE BUDDHIST MONK

—Koestler, A. (1964) *The Act of Creation*

At dawn the monk begins his long ascent,
climbing a narrow Himalayan track
to gain the summit as the light is spent.

A single night in the retreat, then back
at sunrise, drawing near the monastery
step by step with the descending dark.

We might expect, if this were allegory,
some shift during the quiet of his stay,
a realignment of a memory.

But first, a puzzle. Was there along the way,
however quickly or slowly he went,
a place he passed at just the same time each day?

To solve it, disregard the night, invent
a doppelganger monk and synchronise
the journeys. Rather as we might pretend—

teasing each other about destinies—
that our paths crossed before we met. Let's work
the trick with summers in the seventies

when both of us (so we know now) would walk
the same city. Picture us side by side,
negotiating mythical New York.

We almost met when we arrived, wide-eyed,
Grand Central Station. Looking up, we read
the dirty stars. I'm pretty sure you sighed

when I got served in a deli right ahead
of you and stumbled over my order, stunned
by things being various, especially bread.

Remember when I thumbed a book in Strand
and then replaced it on the shelf for you
to find and buy? And didn't we once stand

as close as morning-after lovers do
among the Metropolitan's rooftop sculpture?
We turned our backs on the past to share the view

across the park, the West Side architecture
shining like a model of the future.

CIRCLE

So much to prove
about a line that goes
nowhere,
keeps its distance.

Who doesn't have by heart
the three-syllable poem
of its area,
the music and irony
of that 'squared'?

It's an idea
with a real device
specially made
to describe it.

A device
which can prick
a schoolboy's finger
as well as his curiosity—

the compasses
in his tin of instruments
filled with arcs-
and-circles-in-waiting.

ANIMAL MACABRE

1. The Carousel of Extinct and Endangered Animals

—Dodo Manège, Jardin des Plantes, Paris

The carousel turns slowly in the sun.
The beasts are saddled up for you to ride.
You clamber up the moment that it stops
and pause beside the frilled triceratops
but choose to climb on board the glyptodon,
stroking its knobbly armadillo hide.

And here's the elephant bird or aepyornis,
here's the Tasmanian tiger and the dodo,
the sivatherium with maybe half
the neck of our familiar giraffe.
A panda and gorilla too, to warn us.
Sit tall and smile while papa takes a photo.

2. Statue of Lion and Foot

—Lion Fountain, Jardin des Plantes, Paris
    (Henri Alfred Jacquemart, 1854)

The lion bends its neck as if to sniff
a human foot protruding from the mud.
Severed, perhaps. I choose to think instead
the lion's standing on a buried stiff
with rear paws right above the buried head
of a body it will likely soon uncover
(the toes and heel will make a nice *hors d'oeuvre*).

It's difficult to contemplate this scene
and not conclude the man's unfortunate
that he should whet the lion's appetite.
Which isn't quite correct. The man has been
unlucky, surely. But whatever plight
he faced is hidden from us now—long gone.
All we see here is good luck for the lion.

3. Shop Window with Rats

—*Julien Arouze & Co, Rue des Halles, Paris*

Since 1872, Julien Arouze
has been a pest controller to the stars.
The whole shop-front is splendidly preserved,
yet hard to look at. If you feel unnerved
by all the strung-up rats, why wouldn't you?
The rats are in pristine condition too.
They must have been dunked in formaldehyde
then sunk in alcohol the day they died.
What for? Even if rats are clever critters
it can't be *pour encourager les autres.*
Perhaps they hang, pelts fading in the sun,
to show us this is what we've always done,
help us to carry on. The dead are easier
to kill; killing the living makes us queasier.

ELLIPSE

You know what it is,
but when did you see one
and could you be sure?

There's no formula
for its perimeter.

It's the shape of a planet's orbit,
the shape of our longest journey
cruised on auto-pilot

...

Another year gone?
Didn't feel a thing.

Eccentric circle,
squished/stretched
with two foci, two radii

and two els, though it's easy to miss one.
El slipper, eel slip, slippery fish,

its name from *elleipsis*,
an omission.

TYPO

What the proofs prove
is that there must always exist
more typographical errors
than can be noticed,
even by the most careful scrutineer.

And among the overlooked
is one that confronts the author
the very first time
he opens the published version.

It will ruin his life
although readers might not care,
any more than they care about
the small insults he has already endured
and with which his poems assail them—

the slide-rule
that reminds him of his father's passing,
the woman who turned from him in the rain,
or how he struggles with his herring
in crowded rooms.

PROOFREADING, TRAIN

A print-out covers my seat-back plastic tray.
I'm hopeless at this, however hard I try.

The mind connects, predicts and then expects;
the skittering eye sees what the mind projects.

Outside, the terrace backs with their shabby fences
blithely betray their tenants' confidences.

CUBE

Necker's line-drawing
has two meanings
and you can see them both,
but only one at a time.

It's a kind of poem,
a kind of joke.
Now you don't,
now you get it.

But the joke's on you
and the cube
you see first
is beyond your control.

It's a decision made
by the roll of a die
in your eye's mind.
Which side are you on?

CHAINED LIBRARY & MAPPA MUNDI

—Hereford Cathedral

Good news for a seventeenth-century scholar
who journeyed for months to arrive
in this place of learning and now
consults the plan on the side of the bookcase

to locate *The Hereford Gospels*,
already eight hundred years old. How confident
he can be that it won't be out on loan
or on some trolley in a corner.

It takes both hands and a bit of strength, a heavy clank of iron,
to lower the book to the wooden bench
before he turns to an illuminated page
and reads in the stained-glass light, perhaps a candle to help.

After hours of study, he replaces the volume
spine-first—so easy to imagine it being reopened—
and leaves the chain hanging in its narrow catenary,
its curve of preference, a cobweb thread.

As he leaves, he might consult this vellum map
with its strange symbols, to see how far he has travelled,
to wonder about the sea between England and Scotland,
the snake-eating troglodytes near the Nile

and to consider his next adventures, the places where
he will carry the text in his notes and in his mind,
together with the ideas it has seeded:
perhaps to Jerusalem, in the very centre of the world

or perhaps on his final expedition
to where the map shows Christ and the angels waiting
in what the future will call the 'atmosphere'
and make busy with information.

When the time comes, the scholar decides,
his own name and bones will remain
chained to the earth with his words,
whereas the knowledge he has tended

will keep flowing, like the Nile itself—
new ships hauling their new cargo
along the same ancient watercourse.
And the scholar will mark his departure

with a wave and a serene backward glance,
like the soul on the dappled horse
high-stepping toward the stars
in the southeast quadrant of the chart.

OXBOW

An equilibrium:
its slow evaporation,
speeded by sun and wind,
replenished by the rains.

No flow except this to-
and-fro the weather makes,
the wake of water birds,
the undertow of fish.

TETRAHEDRON

A pyramid
and its name is a bit
like Tutankhamun

but King Tut
was born too late
for a pyramid tomb

and King Tet
isn't the square-based kind
the pharaohs left behind.

The first Platonic solid,
readily defined
as four triangles joined,

it's hard to build
and awkward to hold
and turn in mind

or in the hand.
Its purity's sharp and odd,
nothing aligned.

ANALOGY

If mind is home,
cluttered with junk mail
and stuff you use every day
whether you want to or not

then happiness is a hotel room,
a daydream free of memories
with tomorrow's shirt
hand-washed and drying over the bath.

And locking yourself out of a hotel room
is blip more than blight.
Not so much crisis as comedy.

That time at the conference,
during the small hours of a long night,
when I found myself in the corridor
trying my door in vain, I laughed.
At the mere fact of it, and that I was naked.

All it took to repair the situation
was to tiptoe downstairs
with both hands strategically placed,
and explain to the receptionist
from behind a pot plant.

At home, a similar circumstance,
notwithstanding the dignity of clothing,
has all the elements of a breakdown—
self-blame, panic,
the press of worst-case scenarios
and the search for an open window.

Unless a friend or lover has a key.

MIND, WANDERING

Walking this unfamiliar bridleway,
I'm more than usually mindful of
the here and now, until the very act
of close attention carries me beyond,
to see this ancient track as like a river,
with the steep, wooded bank on either side
and underfoot an exposed bed of stone
worn smooth by generations of travellers
tumbling toward the bay.
                              And when a sunbeam
angles through the autumn sycamores
it picks out Ryan O'Neal as Barry Lyndon,
his horse already stolen, fleeing scandal
to seek his fortune abroad. My turn, perhaps,
to meet a war-widow with whom to spend
a long, disorienting night. My day
to find a flush young lady married to
a frail old lord.
                      Except that I'm with Jen
whose innocent call returns me to the path,
identifying a flower I couldn't name
and birdsong I might not even have noticed.

THE MAN

In a shelter by the road stands a private eye.
A mystery's in his grip, and vice versa.
His reading glasses catch the pages' light.

A hiss of brakes. He lifts that far-sighted gaze.
The bus pulls in, promising
to take him home, by way of other places.

CONE

This is the shape,
the form of the space,
of what can be seen,

with its apex
in the eye of the beholder
and its base and sides
at the limits of vision.

What lies beyond the cone
is outside the bounds
of perception,

too distant
or too peripheral
to be touched by the rays
emitted from the eyes,
according to the model used
in Euclid's *Optics*—

a flawed model,
we now know,
but a metaphor
that allowed Euclid to work,

his searchlight
reaching into the dark.

POEM

The bell on the hat
is a little machine
for remembering its elf.

PARABOLA

Somebody somewhere hurled
the very first snowball—probably a child, or else
an adult suddenly childlike, who aimed high,
intuiting the curve of the flight.

Euclid wrote about this curve,
Apollonius of Perga gave it its name,
Galileo proved it was the shape
of a projectile's path.

Draw it and you can pretend
that the snowball left its mark, like chalk on a board.
You can trace the curve backward, as if the snowball
arced back through time and space

the same way you can pretend
that you're there with them thousands of years ago—
the young, or young at heart, finding a new way to play,
cold but brightly lit, and laughing.

VIE DE JOIE

—Félicien Trewey, 1848–1920

I'm here to shout *hip hip hooray*
for you, Monsieur Trewey.

You spun some plates, Félicien.
Comédien, magicien, musicien

(a multi-instrumentalist,
you made 'em too). Chapeaugraphiste!

Hats off! Lightning sketcher?
—you betcher!

Card scaler! Ace flicker.
Spin that king, throw that joker.

Backwards-writer! Right-to-lefter,
mirroring every first letter.

Balancer! The mad romance
of balleting a static dance.

Shadowgraphiste!
A digital artiste

before your time, casting a panto
of handmade silhouettes. Mime!

Yours a youth that never ended.
Boy, did you misspend it!

CONCRETE POEM

bear with me please
this image calls for
a few hyperboles
the superb figure
luminous against
the ideal screen of
a flawlessly blue sky
as if the cooling tower
were computer graphics
constructed just to clarify
or deepen some mathematics

CROWN GREEN BOWLS

Perhaps
our best, that summer we were young
but played at being old
in whites and daps.
The big exams were done; evenings were long.
Our futures were on hold.

Four boys
killing time on a shaded square
with elms along the side
muffling the noise
from the playground. Grass scent in the air;
the clacks as woods collide.

We set
the bias against the crown, a mark
on the green near the jack for a guide,
or else we let
the effects add, sending the wood on an arc
that seemed impossibly wide.

CYLINDER

Euclid proposed rotating
a rectangle around one of its sides:
The figure so comprehended is a cylinder.
He might have offered a circle
translated along an axis,
but I appreciate his chosen image,
how it hints at roll and wheel. And
I relish that 'comprehend'
though I'd perhaps have said 'generate'
(you might prefer 'describe').
This is something Euclid proved:
description and comprehension
are acts of creation.

STONEY LITTLETON LONG BARROW

And did those feet get raw
climbing the limestone ridge?
Is this the view you saw?
Did you track the same hedge?

Stranger, how come you came?
Was there a burial chamber
murmuring your name?
A passing to remember?

At the entrance, where light
meets dark, did you bend down
to touch the ammonite,
suddenly unalone?

PRISM

The occluded corners,
sides and edges
need to be visible,
so these geometric sketches

of a polyhedron split
into constituent volumes
are transparent,
as if the prisms

Euclid imagined
were made of glass.
Some of them
could split white light

into the rainbow of colours.
Others, when looked through,
would turn the whole world
upside down.

MESSAGE

In the early 19th century, a number of prominent scientists were eager to contact the intelligent life they supposed might inhabit the moon or Mars:

The most widespread version of this story attributes to Gauss the
suggestion that in Siberia there be erected a giant figure in the shape of the
'windmill' diagram used in Euclid's demonstration of the Pythagorean
theorem.

—Crowe, M. J. (1986) *The Extraterrestrial Life Debate 1750-1900*

A right-angled triangle with a square
projecting from each of its three sides
is Euclid's most famous figure.

An astronomer on an outreach mission
(Carl Friedrich Gauss perhaps, 1820-ish)
proposed its deployment

as inter-planetary missive
made of pine forest and wheat field
on the Siberian tundra.

The figure's called a 'windmill'
by scholars referring
to Euclid's proof of Pythagoras's theorem.

It's a bit of a stretch,
a visual metaphor—
a gesture more than a picture.

It can't have looked like a windmill
to Euclid, on his wax-and-stylus
drawing package in sandy Alexandria

and if it were to speak of windmills
to a stargazing Martian
a gloss would be required.

Dear Martian,
(the forest-diagram might say
on behalf of Gauss and us all)

As you peer up
through your planet's thin atmosphere
and wonder about us

we sit at our desks listening
to the wind shaking
the pine trees and the wheat.

We know how
to borrow wind's power
to grind the harvested grain.

We understand scale.
We worry about style,
form and rule.

Friend, our machines
might not work for you but
here is our geometry.

Yours truly ...

THE NYLON TENT

—after Robert Frost

He is as in a street a nylon tent
at midnight when the bitter winter snow
has iced the cobbles and its zippered vent
for regulating water vapour flow
is, even in this cold, undone a peep
and signifies, perhaps, a breathy moan
escaping from the open mouth of sleep
over a groundsheet on the paving stone
that offers no fit place for pegging down
but means it must instead be ballasted
with worldly goods or bricks from round the town,
and every time its walls get buffeted
by the ungodly blasts of winter air
is of these slight foundations made aware.

SPHERE

An ideal so attractive
we see it in nature's rough tries.
Think eyeball, or blueberry.

At a different scale,
there's earth and its moon,
the planets and stars,
heavenly almost-spheres
that move like a string or a bell
and so make music
too deep for us to hear,
according to Pythagoras,
who himself played the lute
as well as the triangle.

And there are the nearly-spheres
we engineer, the beach balls
with their puffed-up panels,
tennis balls with that channel
through the fluff,
and rolled-out foodstuff,
truffles and falafels.

Nothing's perfect.
Although a soap bubble
is as impeccable
as it's ephemeral,
its vanishing almost audible.

VITREOUS

Blank page, scourge of writers,
showing me only these squirms of detritus

about myself. I scatter them in
the bright café: its latte women,

each the star of a story,
the momentary mystery

of a cardigan draped on a chair,
the ceiling fan dealing the air

a cut of the flow and fuss,
and on the page, flaws in my glass.

ABOUT THE AUTHOR

Stephen Payne is a Professor Emeritus at the University of Bath, where until September 2020 he taught in the Department of Computer Science and supervised research on Cognitive Science and Human-Computer Interaction. He lives in Penarth in the Vale of Glamorgan. This is his second full collection—the first, *Pattern Beyond Chance*, was shortlisted for the Wales Book of the Year Award, 2016.